curious about

CANOEING

BY RACHEL GRACK

AMICUS LEARNING

What are you

curious about?

Curious about is published by
Amicus Learning, an imprint of Amicus
P.O. Box 227
Mankato, MN 56002
www.amicuspublishing.us

Editor: Alissa Thielges
Series Designer: Kathleen Petelinsek
Book Designer: Aubrey Harper

Library of Congress Cataloging-in-Publication Data
Names: Koestler-Grack, Rachel A., 1973- author.
Title: Curious about canoeing / by Rachel Grack.
Description: Mankato, MN: Amicus Learning, 2024. | Series: Curious about the great outdoors | Includes bibliographical references and index. | Audience: Ages 5–9 | Audience: Grades 2–3 | Summary: "Questions and answers give kids the fundamentals of canoeing, including gear and where to canoe. Includes infographics to support visual learning and back matter to support research skills, plus glossary and index"—Provided by publisher.
Identifiers: LCCN 2023011710 (print) | LCCN 2023011711 (ebook) | ISBN 9781645496588 (library binding) | ISBN 9781681529479 (paperback) | ISBN 9781645496847 (pdf)
Subjects: LCSH: Canoes and canoeing—Juvenile literature.
Classification: LCC GV784.3 .K (print) | LCC GV784.3 (ebook) | DDC 797.122—dc23/eng/20230313
LC record available at https://lccn.loc.gov/2023011710
LC ebook record available at https://lccn.loc.gov/2023011711

Photo credits: Alamy/Design Pics Inc, 13, Hero Images Inc., 18; Corbis/Cecepr, 11; iStock/ADragan, 17, claylib, 17, DonNichols, 17, FatCamera, 6–7, gulfix, 17, Hero Images, 12, ImagineGolf, 14–15, 16, prapann, 17, sianc, 21, Tom Merton, 19; Shutterstock/marekuliasz, 11, marekuliasz, 8, New Africa, 8, sianc, cover, 1; SuperStock/dotshock, 5; Unsplash/Atia Naim, 8

Printed in China

CHAPTER ONE

Why do people canoe?

Many people go canoeing for fun. They get out on the water and enjoy nature. It's great exercise, too. Some use their canoes to go fishing. Others canoe as a sport. They do **sprint** and **slalom** races. Canoeing is even an Olympic event.

Many parks have canoes you can borrow or rent.

DID YOU KNOW?
The world's oldest boat is a canoe. It's from 10,000 years ago!

Is canoeing hard?

Canoeing is easier and more fun to learn with others.

Only if you go alone. **Tandem** canoeing is best for beginners. Two paddlers keep the canoe straight and steady. You can take a canoeing class. But most people teach themselves. It just takes a little practice. Grab a friend and give it a try!

DID YOU KNOW?
Canoes tip easier than other boats. It is a good idea to learn how to swim before you go canoeing.

Are canoes and kayaks the same?

Canoes are good for long trips in the wilderness.

No. Canoes are bigger than kayaks. Canoes have open tops with bench seats. There is more space to carry gear for a trip. Kayaks have closed tops. The paddles are different, too. Kayakers use a double paddle. This has a blade on both ends. Most people use single paddles to canoe.

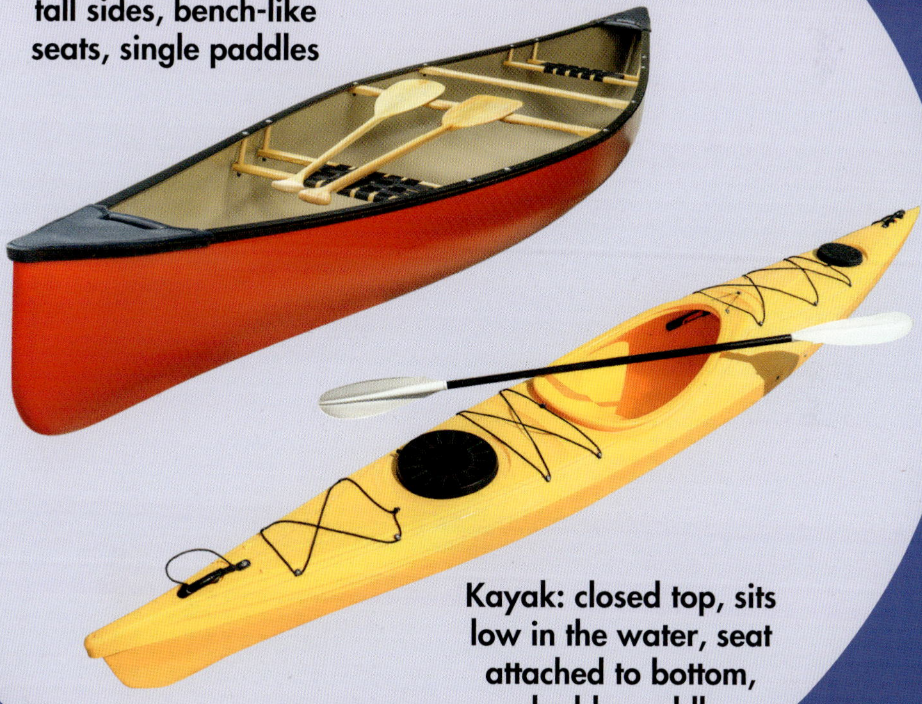

CANOE VS. KAYAK

CHAPTER TWO

How do I get a canoe?

Many people rent one. Canoe rental shops know the best boats for beginners. Wide, flat-bottom canoes are least likely to tip over. Shorter canoes are easier to paddle and steer. Canoes made of **aluminum** are popular. They are very sturdy.

Plastic canoes are lighter than metal ones.

PARTS OF A CANOE

Bow: front of canoe

Gunwales: top edge of hull

Stern: back of canoe

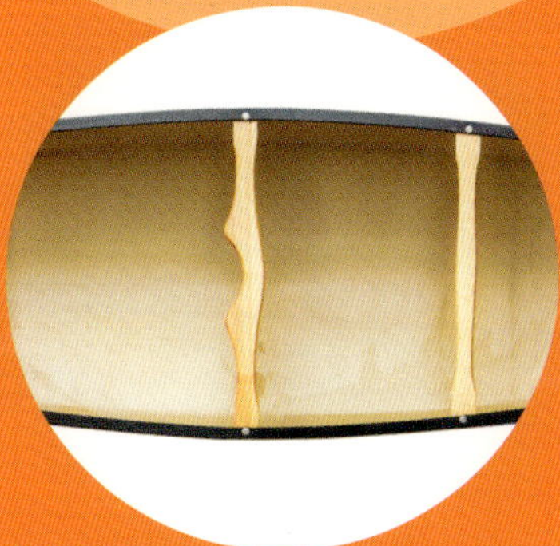

Hull: body of canoe

Keel: outer bottom ridge that runs from bow to stern

Canoeing on a lake can be a fun summer activity.

Where can I canoe?

Anywhere water is deep enough! Go canoeing on lakes, rivers, and streams. Beginners should stick to still or slow-moving water. Pay attention to the weather, too. Water gets choppy on a windy day. But some people like a bumpy ride. They go canoeing on **whitewater rapids**.

Whitewater canoeing is risky and exciting.

Which paddle should I use?

The stronger paddler sits in the back and steers the boat.

First, find the right length. There are different ways to measure. One way is to stand the paddles in front of you. The one even with your eyes is a good size. Front paddlers sometimes use bent paddles. Straight paddles work best at the **stern**.

What do I wear?

The paddles sometimes splash, so be prepared to get wet.

Always wear a life jacket! Otherwise, dress for the weather and water. Wear a t-shirt and shorts or a swimsuit on a hot day. Put on warmer clothes for cool weather or cold water. Choose clothing that dries fast. Water shoes or rubber boots with good grip keep feet dry and steady. Whitewater canoers often wear **dry suits** and helmets.

SUNSCREEN

BUG SPRAY

HAT

WATER BOTTLE

COOLER

CHAPTER THREE

People fish in a canoe in the middle of lakes.

How do I get in?

Near shore or next to a dock. Always use three points of **contact**. Step into the middle of the canoe. Hold onto both sides of the boat if possible. Otherwise, the canoe could tip over. The first time feels tricky. You or your gear might fall out. But don't quit. Dry off and try again!

Have one person hold the canoe steady as you get in.

What if my canoe tips over?

Hold onto your canoe! It will help you stay afloat. Climb on top and wait for help. Never leave your canoe to swim to shore.

Sometimes canoes tip but do not **capsize**. Whew! But now there's water inside. Use a **bilge pump** or sponges to empty it out. Paddle on!

HOW TO STOP A TIPPING CANOE

Do not grab the gunwales.

Sit down.

Put your paddle in the water.

ASK MORE QUESTIONS

Where can I rent a canoe?

What is the best paddle stroke?

Try a BIG QUESTION: Would I like canoeing or kayaking better?

SEARCH FOR ANSWERS

Search the library catalog or the Internet.
A librarian, teacher, or parent can help you.

Using Keywords
Find the looking glass.

Keywords are the most important words in your question.

If you want to know:

- how to find canoe rentals near you, type: RENT CANOES IN [YOUR CITY]
- about paddle strokes, type: CANOEING PADDLE STROKES

LEARN MORE

FIND GOOD SOURCES

Here are some good, safe sources you can use in your research.
Your librarian can help you find more.

Books

Canoeing
by Lisa Owings, 2023.

Go Canoeing
by Nicole A. Mansfield, 2023.

Internet Sites

American Canoe Association
https://americancanoe.org
The American Canoe Association website is a source for canoeing and other paddle sports. Find classes and other information for youth canoeing.

Kids Britannica: Canoeing
https://kids.britannica.com/students/article/canoeing/273491
Kids Britannica is an online encyclopedia for kids. Learn about the history of canoeing.

Every effort has been made to ensure that these websites are appropriate for children. However, because of the nature of the Internet, it is impossible to guarantee that these sites will remain active indefinitely or that their contents will not be altered.

SHARE AND TAKE ACTION

Take a canoeing class.
Learn canoeing basics before hitting the water.

Join a canoeing club.
Find a local canoeing club and meet new paddling friends!

Organize a canoeing trip.
Ask family and friends to go canoeing with you.

GLOSSARY

aluminum A silver metal that is strong and light.

bilge pump A handpump used to pump water out of a boat.

capsize To flip upside down.

contact The state of touching something.

dry suit A tight piece of clothing that covers the body and keeps out water.

slalom A canoe race on choppy waters where contestants have to paddle through gates on a course.

sprint A canoe race on calm waters.

stern The back of a boat.

tandem A group of two people who work together.

whitewater rapids Choppy, fast-moving water on a river.

INDEX

About the Author

Rachel Grack has been editing and writing children's books since 1999. She lives in Arizona, a state where the great outdoors offers countless adventures all year long. Horseback riding has been one of her favorite outdoor activities. But geocaching might be her next big adventure.